2017 Calendar – Japan Outdoor & Nature Photos – U.S.A. Version

(United States National Holidays Shown)
(Full Moon Dates = ☺)

Copyright © 2016 Daniel H. Wieczorek & Kazuya Numazawa

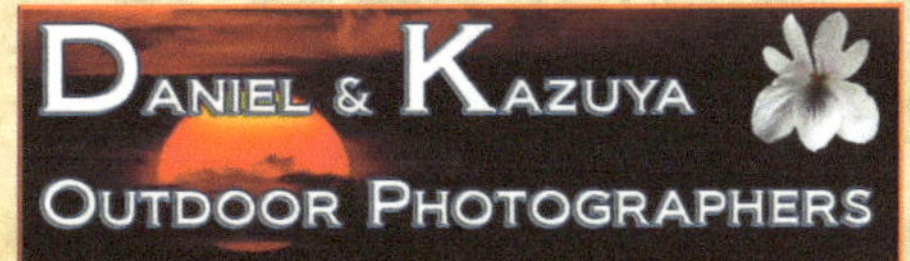

ISBN-10: 0-9969810-1-2
ISBN-13: 978-0-9969810-1-9

PHOTOS INCLUDED IN THIS CALENDAR

January: A snowy stream near Tsuru No Yu (The Hot Spring of the Crane) in Akita Prefecture, Japan.
February: An amazing Skunk Cabbage (*Symplocarpus foetidus*) blossom in Nogawa Park, Mitaka, Tokyo, Japan.
March: Two *Viola eizanensis* flowers near Mt. Takao, Tokyo, Japan.
April: A Takao Violet (*Viola yezoensis* f. *discolor*) blossom near Mt. Takao, Tokyo, Japan.
May: Nishizawa (West Creek) and waterfalls, Yamanashi Prefecture, Japan.
June: Mt. Fuji from near the boundary of Shizuoka and Yamanashi Prefectures, Japan.
July: A Lotus blossom from below. Jindai Botanical Garden, Mitaka, Tokyo, Japan.
August: Mt. Hiuchigatake & Oze Pond, Oze National Park. Fukushima Prefecture, Japan.
September: An Iwa Hiba (Spike Moss) specimen at Jindai Botanical Garden, Mitaka, Tokyo, Japan.
October: A scene in Moomin Valley, Mt. Akita-Komagatake, Akita Prefecture, Japan.
November: An amazingly bright red maple on Mt. Akita-Komagatake, Akita Prefecture, Japan.
December: "Diamond Fuji" – the day the sun sets behind Mt. Fuji – taken from the summit of Mt. Takao, Tokyo, Japan.

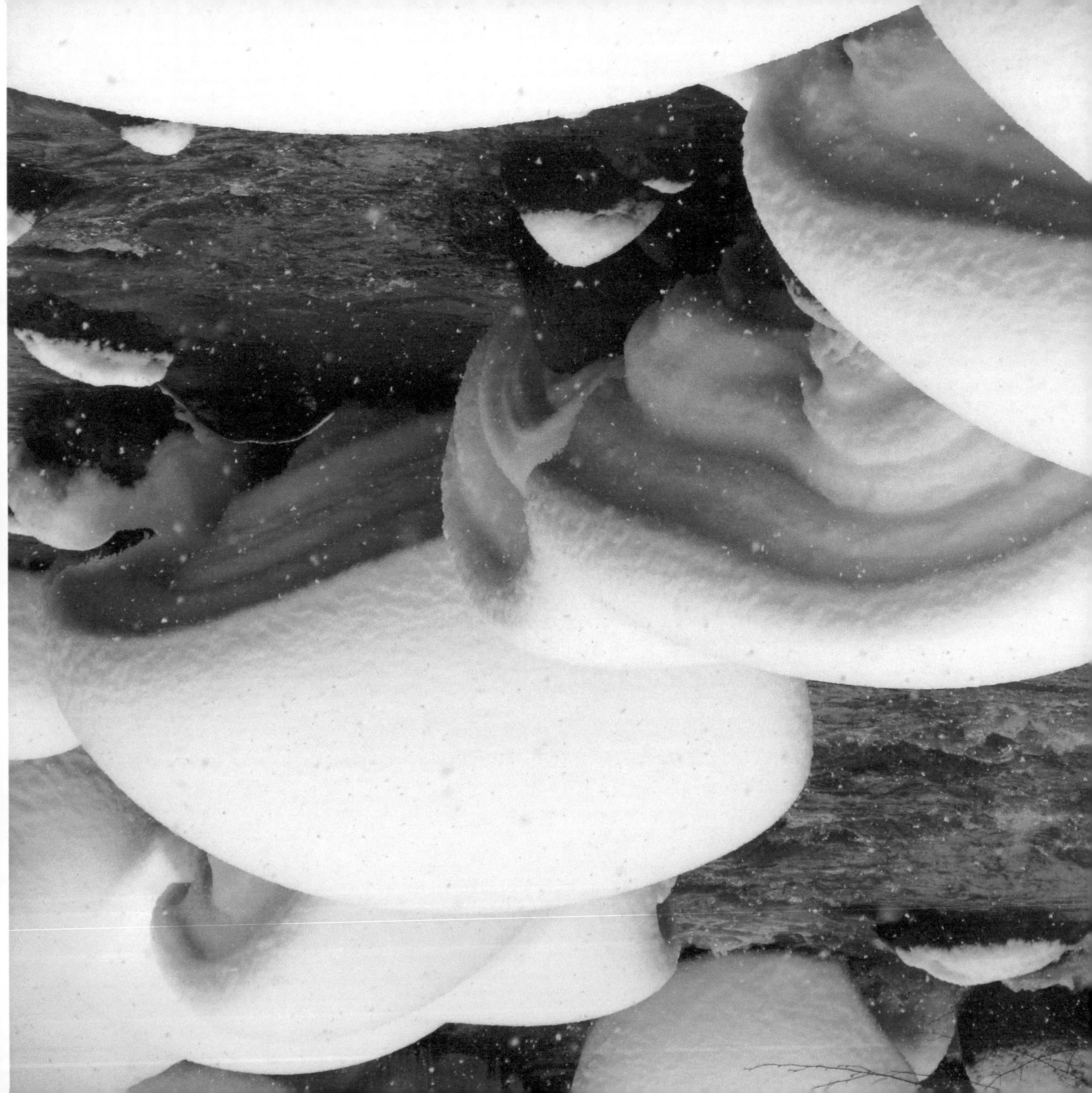

January 2017

Sun	Mon	Tue	Wed	Thu	Fri	Sat
25	26	27	28	29	30	31
1 New Year's Day	2 New Year's Day observed	3	4	5	6	7
8	9	10	11	13	14	
15	16 Martin Luther King Day	17	18	19	20	21
22	23	24	25	26	27	28
29	30	31	1	2	3	4

A snowy stream near Tsuru No Yu (The Hot Spring of the Crane) in Akita Prefecture, Japan.

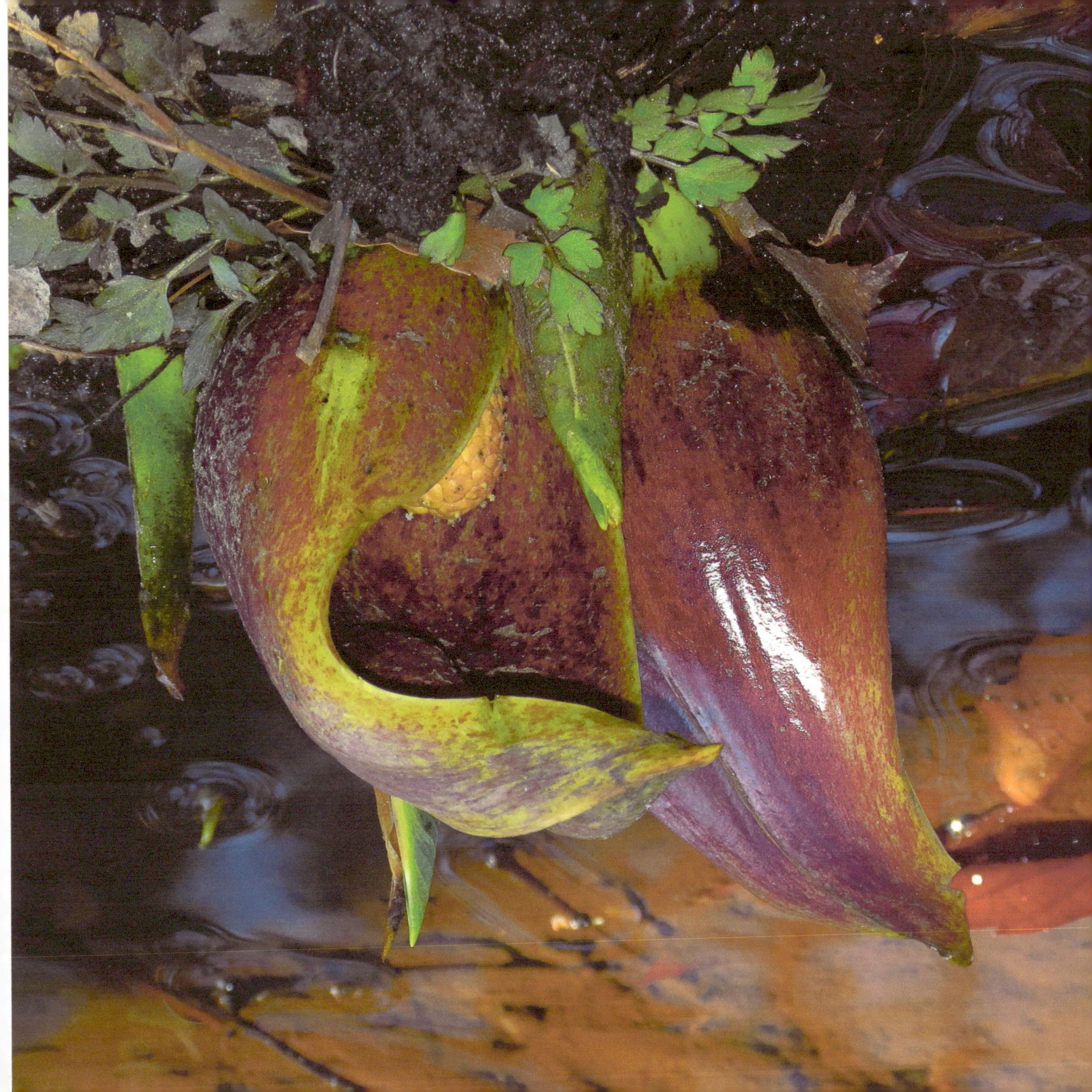

February 2017

Sun	Mon	Tue	Wed	Thu	Fri	Sat
29	30	31	1	2	3	4
5	6	7	8	9	☺	11
12	13	14 Valentine's Day	15	16	17	18
19	20 President's Day	21	22	23	24	25
26	27	28	1	2	3	4

An amazing Skunk Cabbage (*Symplocarpus foetidus*) blossom in Nogawa Park, Mitaka, Tokyo, Japan.

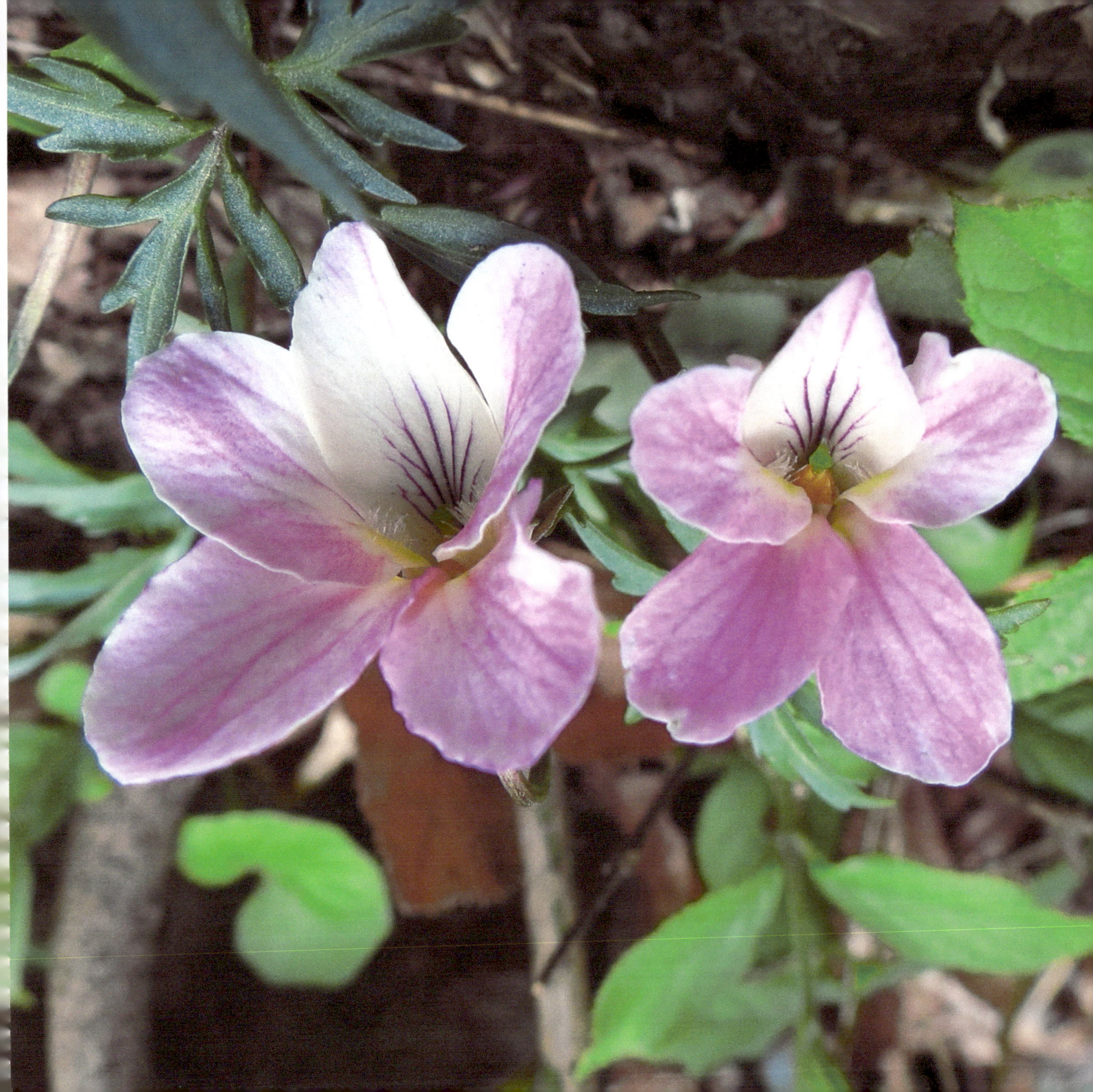

<table>
<thead>
<tr><th>March</th><th></th><th></th><th></th><th></th><th></th><th>2017</th></tr>
<tr><th>Sun</th><th>Mon</th><th>Tue</th><th>Wed</th><th>Thu</th><th>Fri</th><th>Sat</th></tr>
</thead>
<tbody>
<tr><td>26</td><td>27</td><td>28</td><td>1</td><td>2</td><td>3</td><td>4</td></tr>
<tr><td>5</td><td>6</td><td>7</td><td>8</td><td>9</td><td>10</td><td>11</td></tr>
<tr><td>12
Daylight Saving Time Begin (02:00)</td><td>13</td><td>14</td><td>15</td><td>16</td><td>17</td><td>18</td></tr>
<tr><td>19</td><td>20
10:29 GMT
Vernal Equinox</td><td>21</td><td>22</td><td>23</td><td>24</td><td>25</td></tr>
<tr><td>26</td><td>27</td><td>28</td><td>29</td><td>30</td><td>31</td><td>1</td></tr>
</tbody>
</table>

Two *Viola eizanensis* flowers near Mt. Takao, Tokyo, Japan.

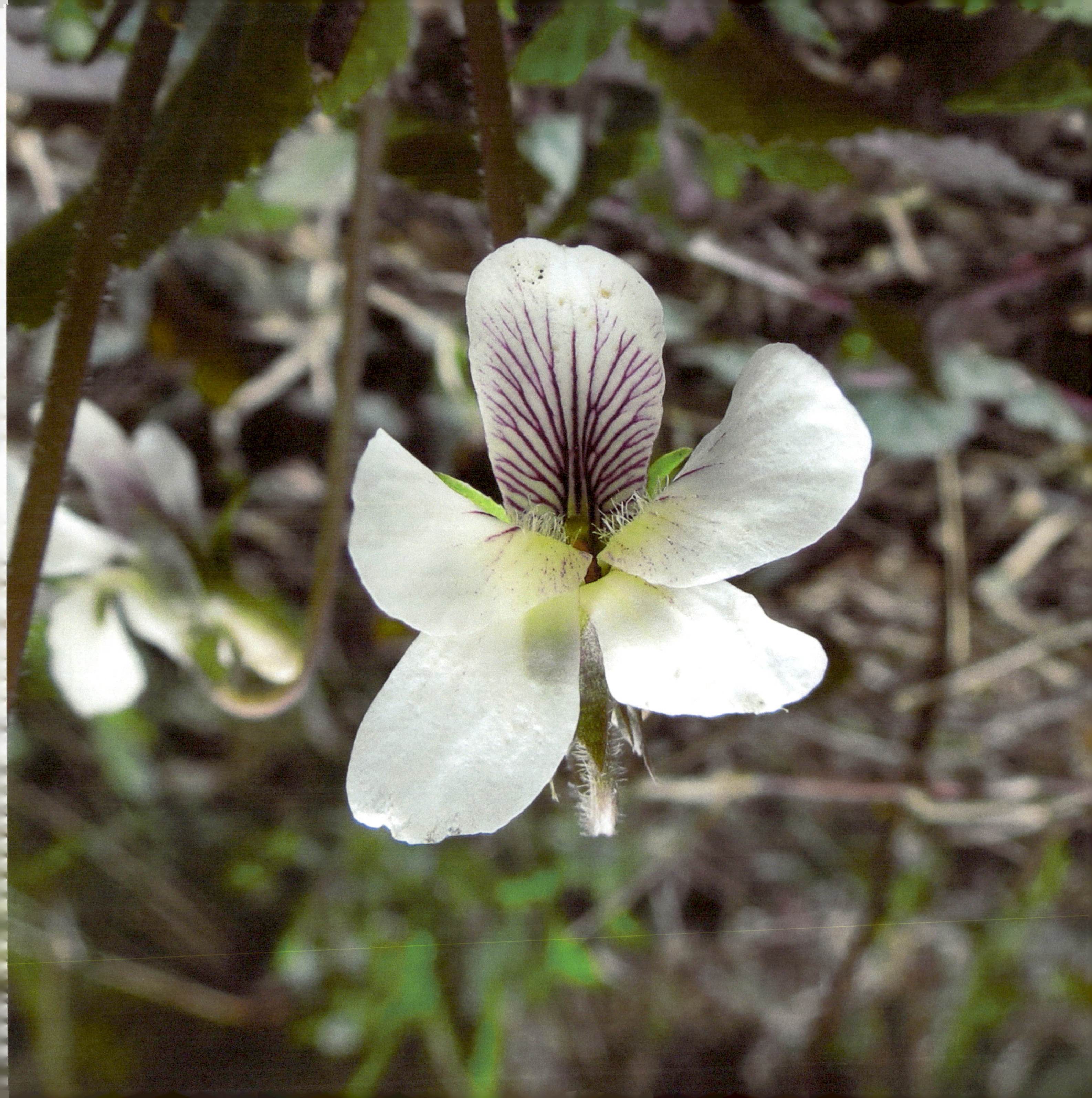

April 2017

Sun	Mon	Tue	Wed	Thu	Fri	Sat
26	27	28	29	30	31	1
2	3	4	5	6	7	8
9	10		12	13	14	15
16 Easter Sunday	17	18	19	20	21	22
23	24	25	26	27	28	29
30	1	2	3	4	5	6

A Takao Violet (*Viola yezoensis f. discolor*) blossom near Mt. Takao, Tokyo, Japan.

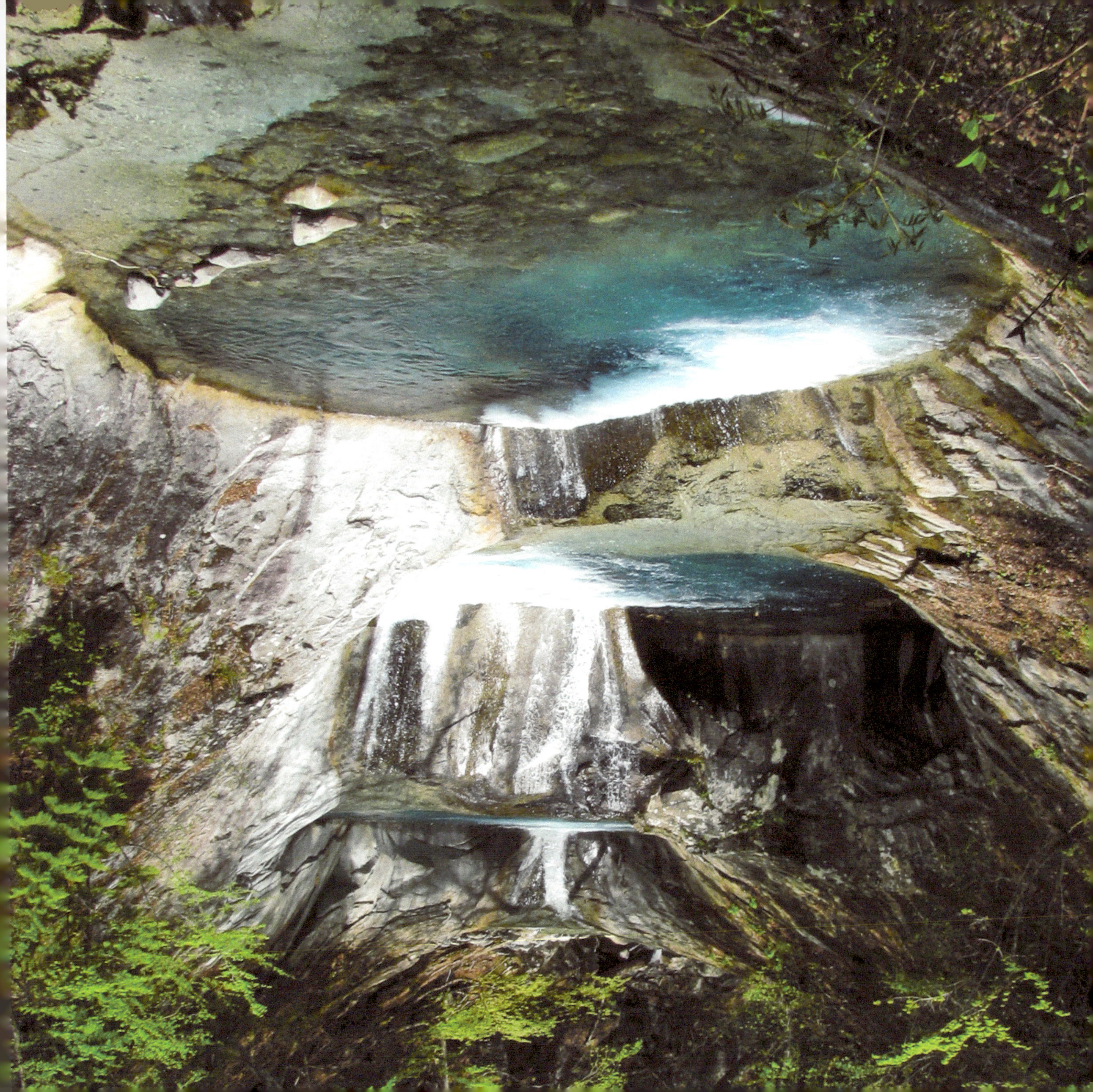

May 2017

Sun	Mon	Tue	Wed	Thu	Fri	Sat
30	1	2	3	4	5	6
7	8	9	☺	11	12	13
14 Mother's Day	15	16	17	18	19	20
21	22	23	24	25	26	27
28	29 Memorial Day	30	31	1	2	3

Nishizawa (West Creek) and waterfalls, Yamanashi Prefecture, Japan.

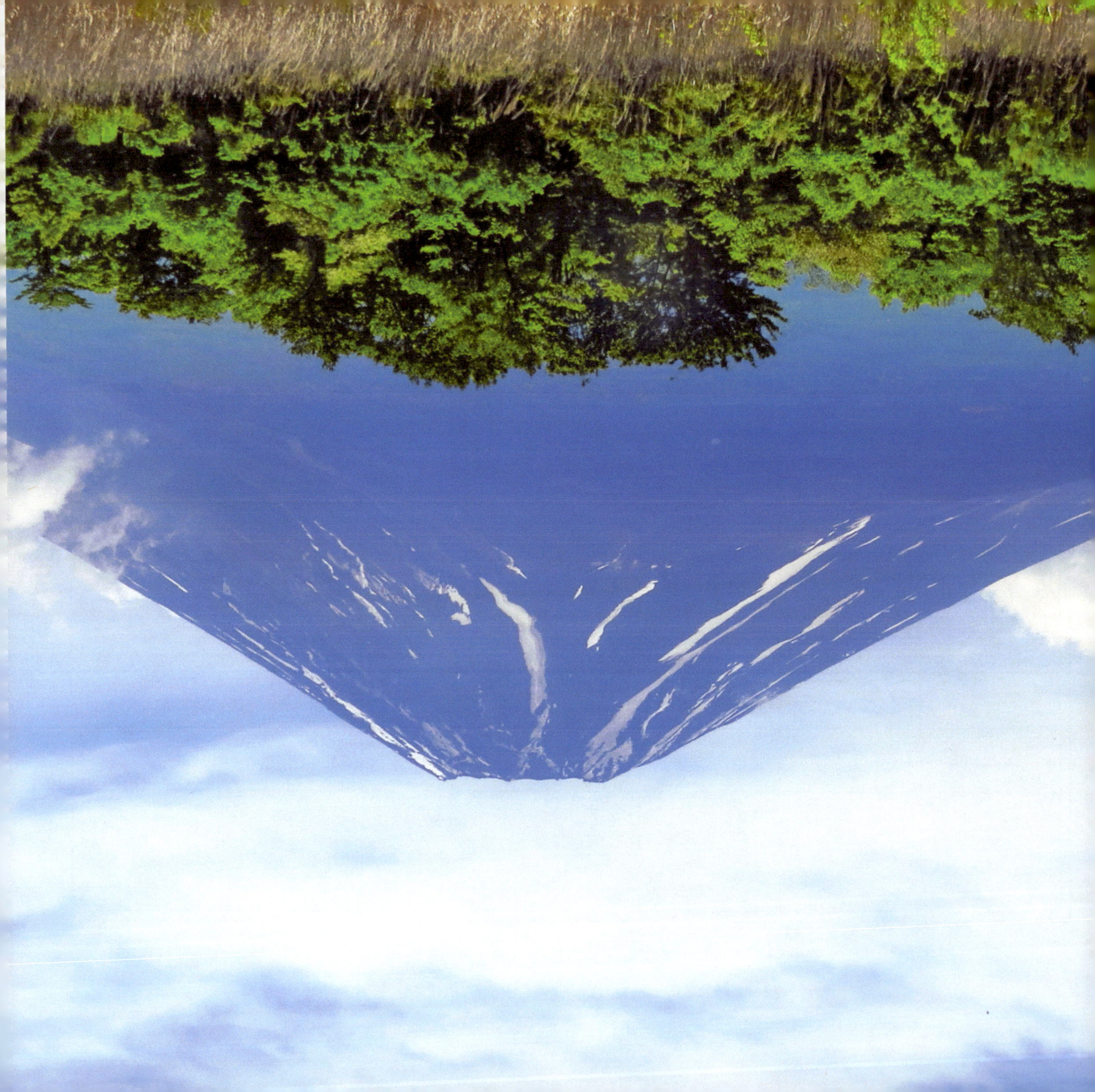

June 2017

Sun	Mon	Tue	Wed	Thu	Fri	Sat
28	29	30	31	1	2	3
4	5	6	7	8	☺	10
11	12	13	14	15	16	17
18 Father's Day	19	20	21 04:24 GMT Summer Solstice	22	23	24
25	26	27	28	29	30	1

Mt. Fuji from near the boundary of Shizuoka and Yamanashi Prefectures, Japan.

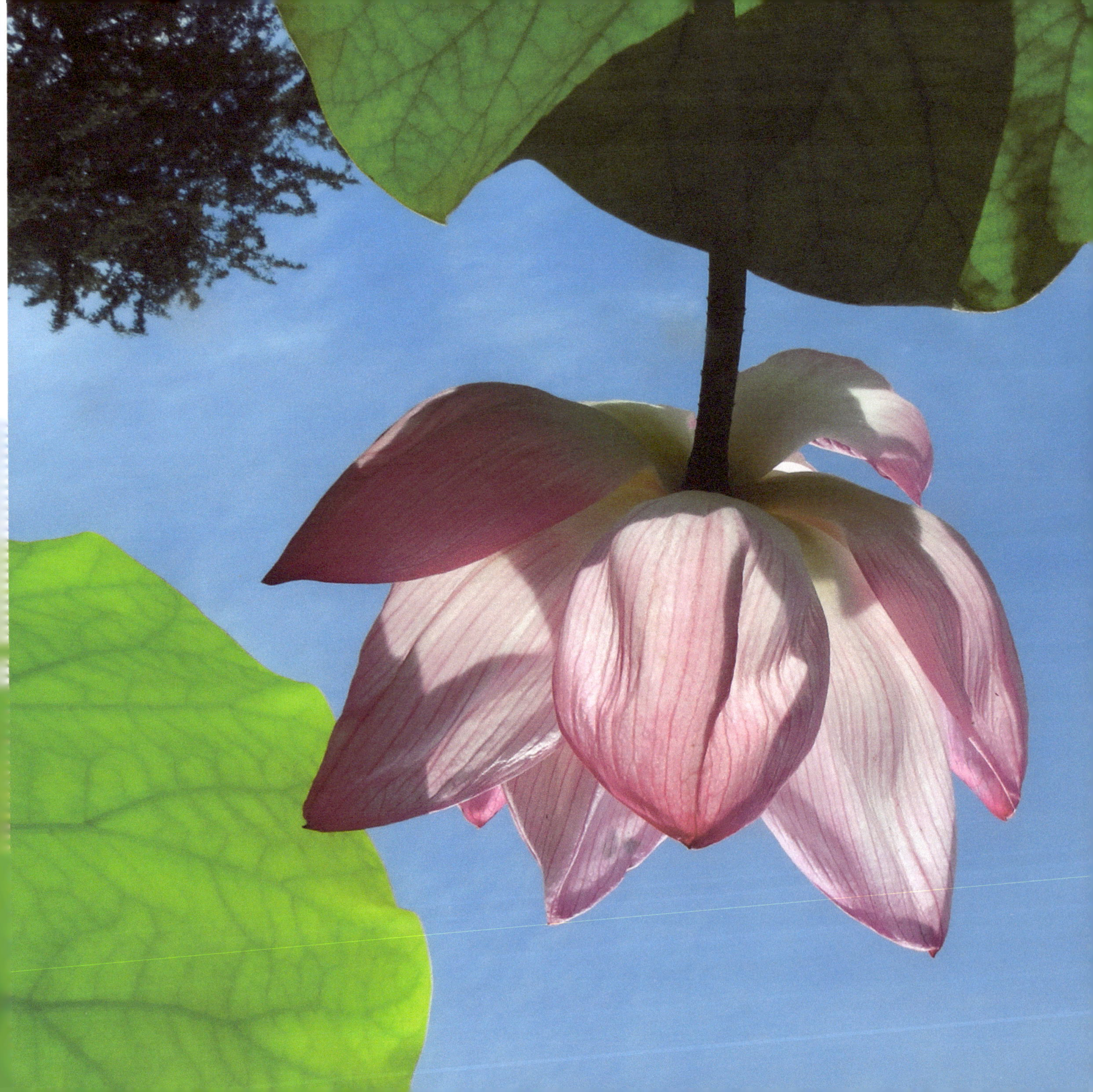

July 2017

Sun	Mon	Tue	Wed	Thu	Fri	Sat
25	26	27	28	29	30	1
2	3	4 Independence Day	5	6	7	8
9	10	11	12	13	14	15
16	17	18	19	20	21	22
23	24	25	26	27	28	29
30	31	1	2	3	4	5

A Lotus blossom from below. Jindai Botanical Garden, Mitaka, Tokyo, Japan.

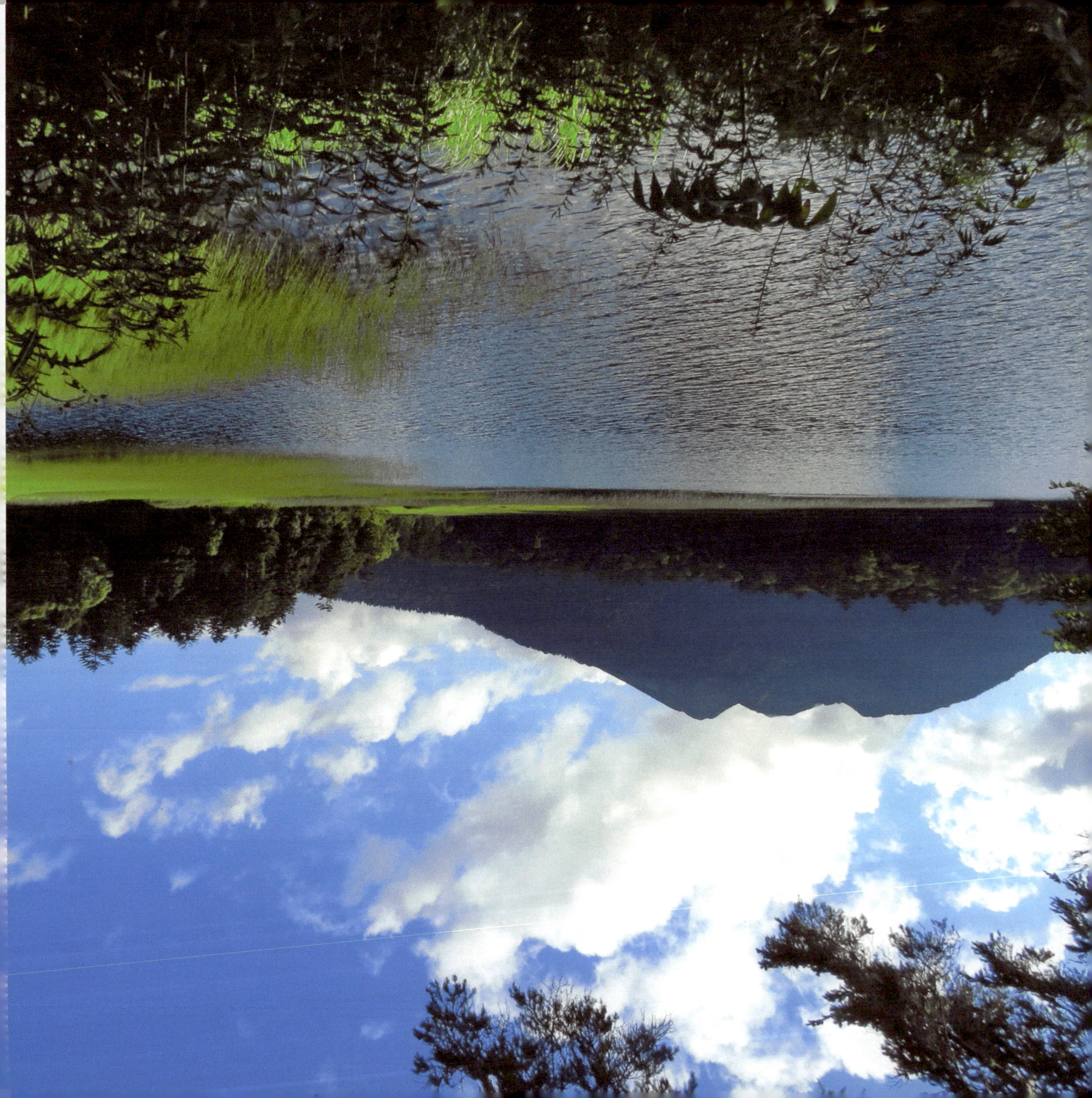

Sun	Mon	Tue	Wed	Thu	Fri	Sat
30	31	1	2	3	4	5
6	☺	8	9	10	11	12
13	14	15	16	17	18	19
20	21	22	23	24	25	26
27	28	29	30	31	1	2

Mt. Hiuchigatake & Oze Pond, Oze National Park. Fukushima Prefecture, Japan.

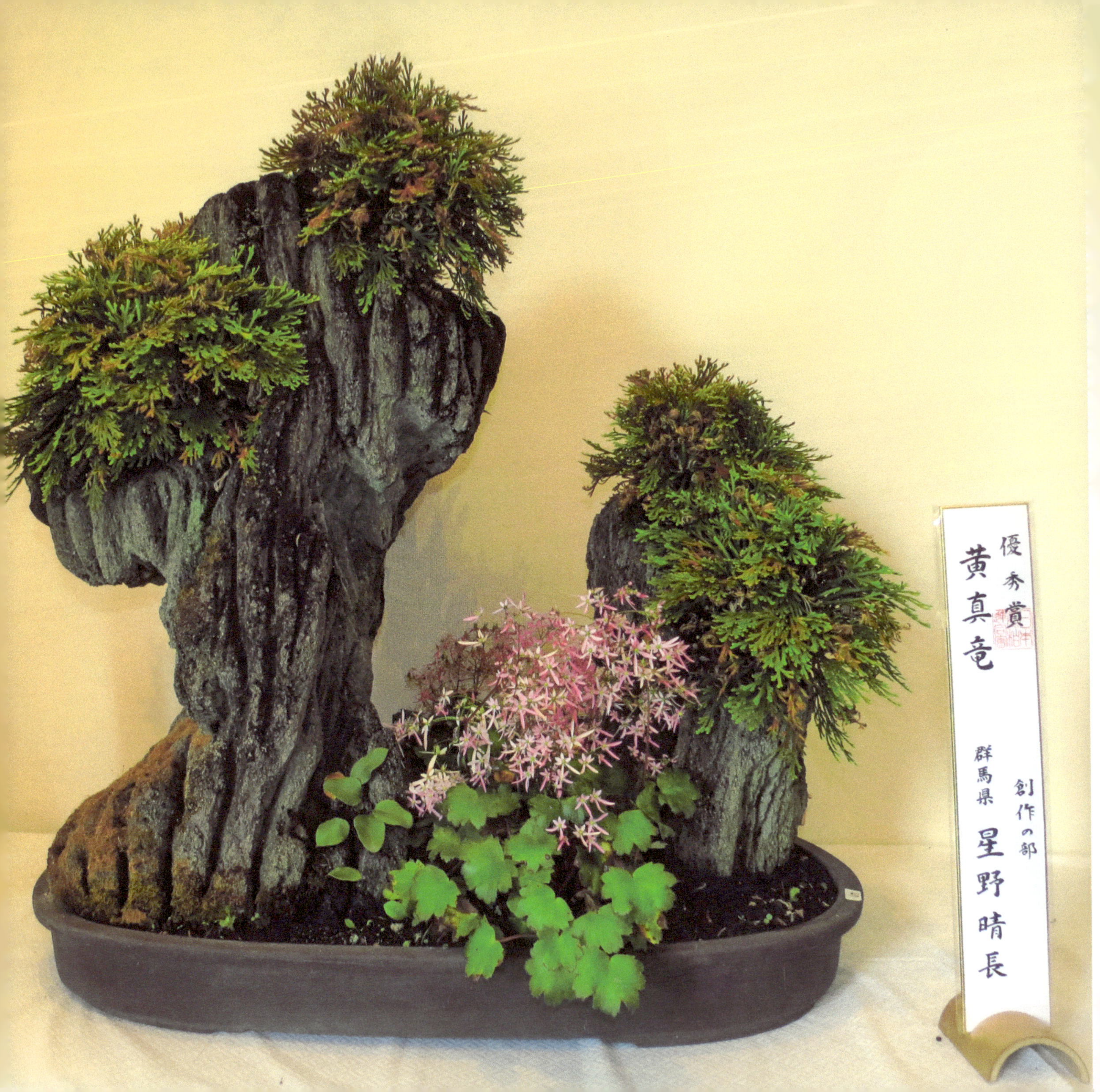

September 2017

Sun	Mon	Tue	Wed	Thu	Fri	Sat
27	28	29	30	31	1	2
3	4 Labor Day	5	☺	7	8	9
10	11	12	13	14	15	16
17	18	19	20	21	22 20:02 GMT Autumnal Equinox	23
24	25	26	27	28	29	30

An Iwa Hiba (Spike Moss) specimen at Jindai Botanical Garden, Mitaka, Tokyo, Japan.

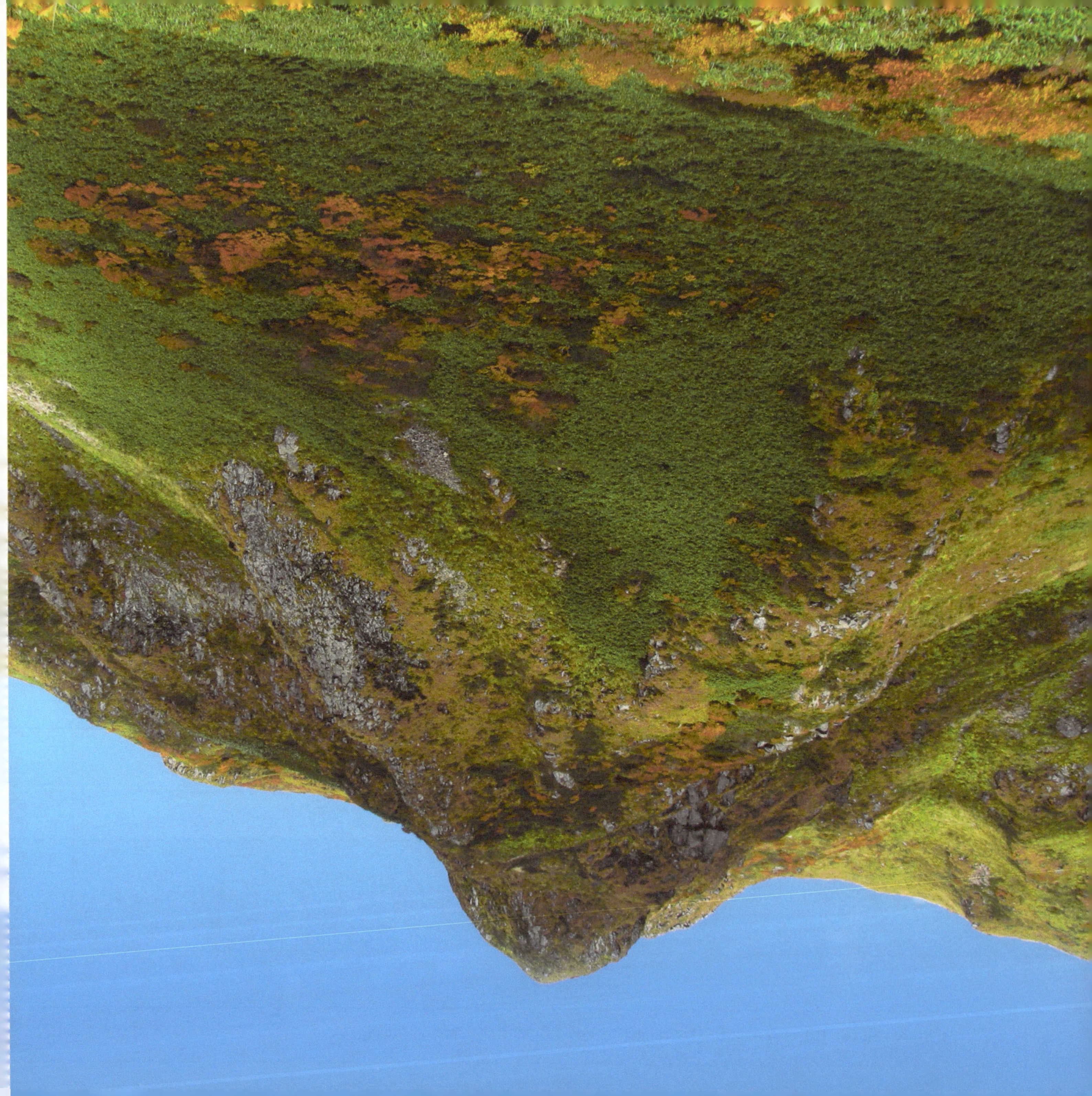

October 2017

Sun	Mon	Tue	Wed	Thu	Fri	Sat
1	2	3	4	☺	6	7
8	9 Columbus Day	10	11	12	13	14
15	16	17	18	19	20	21
22	23	24	25	26	27	28
29	30	31 Halloween	1	2	3	4

A scene in Moomin Valley, Mt. Akita-Komagatake, Akita Prefecture, Japan.

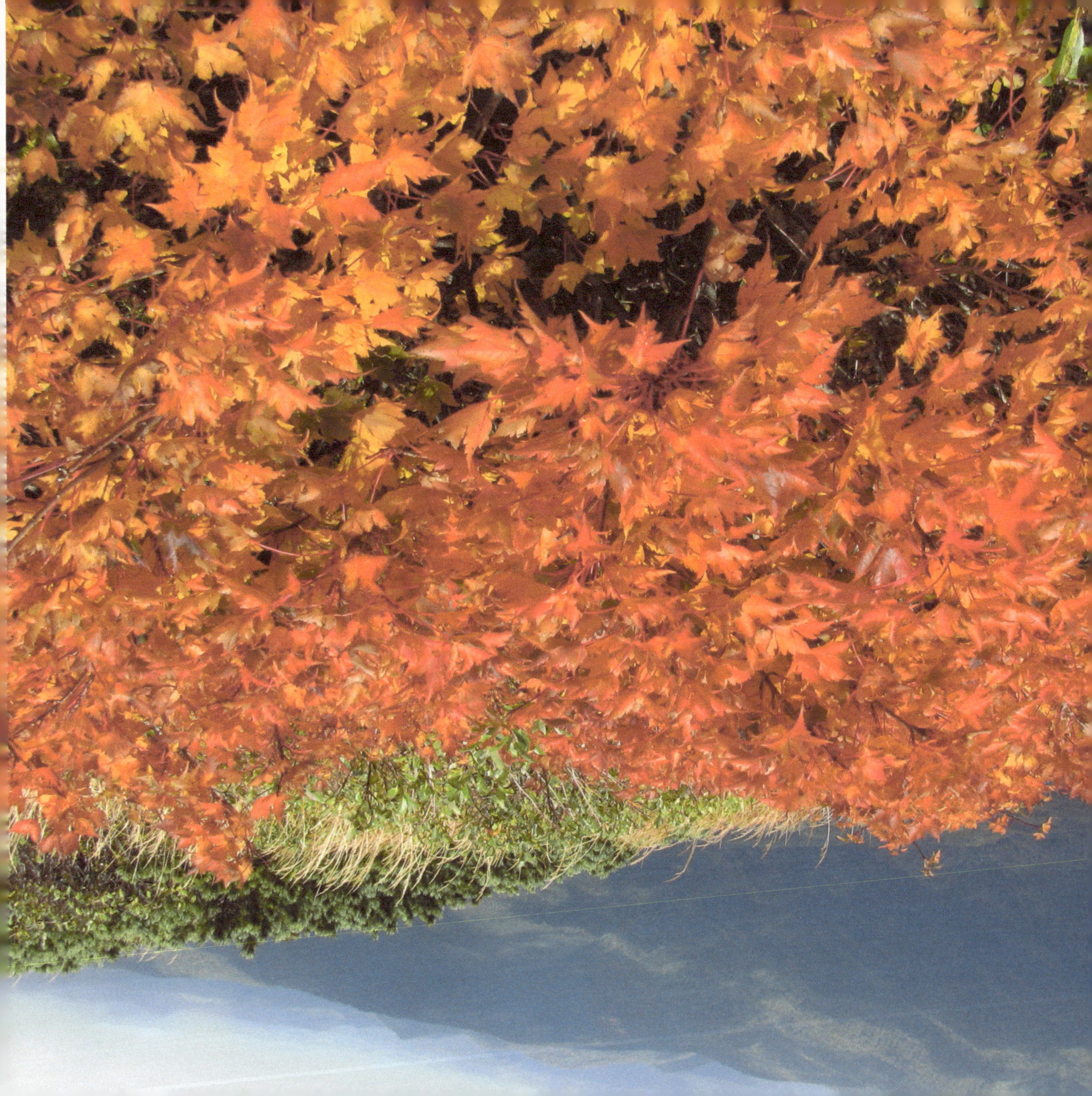

November 2017

Sun	Mon	Tue	Wed	Thu	Fri	Sat
29	30	31	1	2	3	
5 Daylight Saving Time End (02:00)	6	7	8	9	10	11 Veteran's Day
12	13	14	15	16	17	18
19	20	21	22	23 Thanksgiving Day	24	25
26	27	28	29	30	1	2

An amazingly bright red maple on Mt. Akita-Komagatake, Akita Prefecture, Japan.

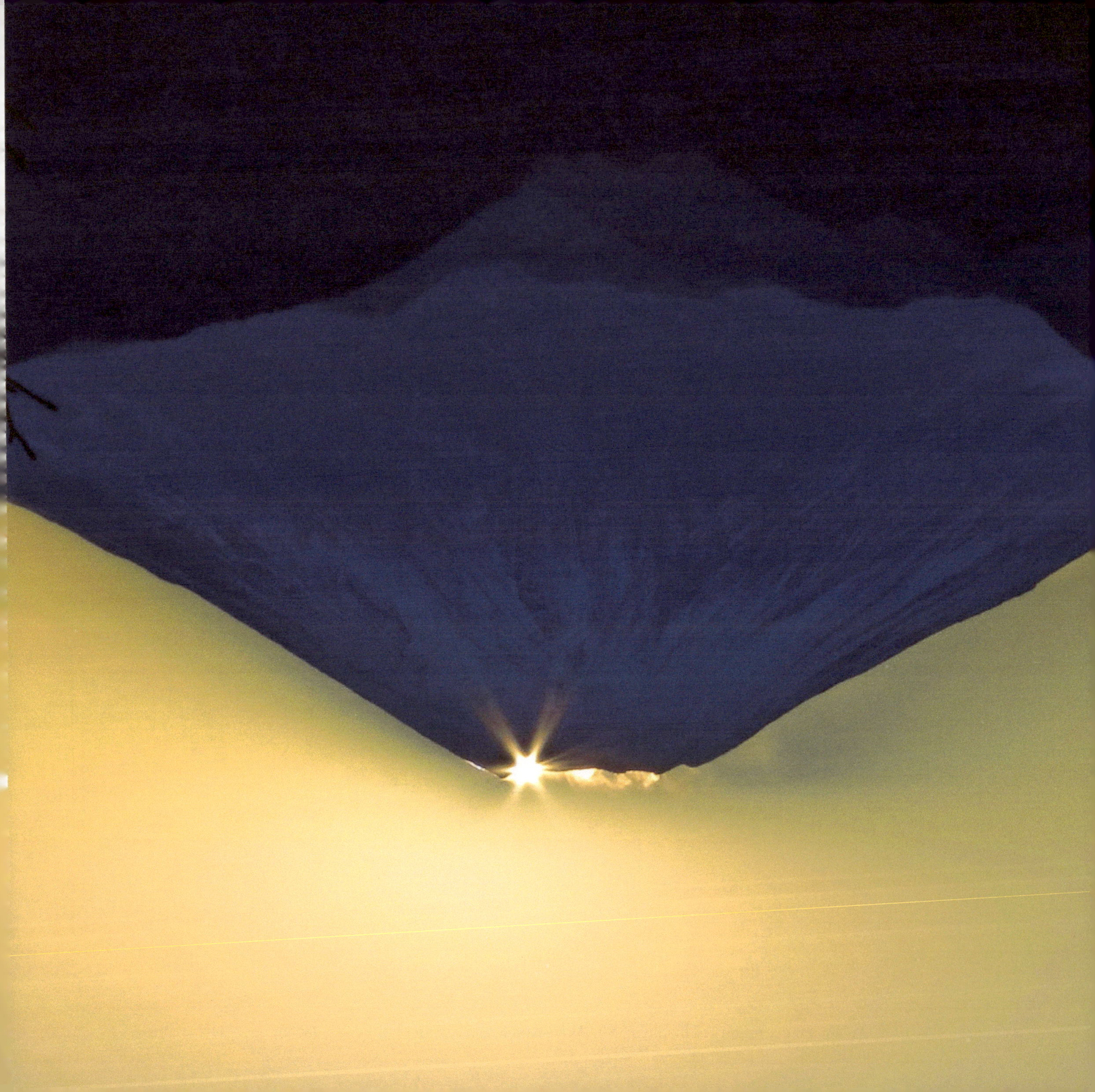

Sun	Mon	Tue	Wed	Thu	Fri	Sat
26	27	28	29	30	1	2
	4	5	6	7	8	9
10	11	12	13	14	15	16
17	18	19	20	21 16:28 GMT Winter Solstice	22	23
24 Christmas Eve	25 Christmas Day	26	27	28	29	30
31 New Year's Eve	1	2	3	4	5	6

"Diamond Fuji" – the day the sun sets behind Mt. Fuji – taken from the summit of Mt. Takao, Tokyo, Japan.

2017 Phases of the Moon

Universal Time (GMT)

New Moon				First Quarter				Full Moon				Last Quarter			
	d	h	m		d	h	m		d	h	m		d	h	m
—	—	—	—	JAN	05	19	47	JAN	12	11	34	JAN	19	22	13
JAN	28	00	07	FEB	04	04	19	FEB	11	00	33	FEB	18	19	33
FEB	26	14	58	MAR	05	11	32	MAR	12	14	54	MAR	20	15	58
MAR	28	02	57	APR	03	18	39	APR	11	06	08	APR	19	09	57
APR	26	12	16	MAY	03	02	47	MAY	10	21	42	MAY	19	00	33
MAY	25	19	44	JUN	01	12	42	JUN	09	13	10	JUN	17	11	33
JUN	24	02	31	JUL	01	00	51	JUL	09	04	07	JUL	16	19	26
JUL	23	09	46	JUL	30	15	23	AUG	07	18	11	AUG	15	01	15
AUG	21	18	30	AUG	29	08	13	SEP	06	07	03	SEP	13	06	25
SEP	20	05	30	SEP	28	02	53	OCT	05	18	40	OCT	12	12	25
OCT	19	19	12	OCT	27	22	22	NOV	04	05	23	NOV	10	20	36
NOV	18	11	42	NOV	26	17	03	DEC	03	15	47	DEC	10	07	51
DEC	18	06	30	DEC	26	09	20	—	—	—	—	—	—	—	—

Earth's Seasons – 2017

Universal Time (GMT)

		d	h			d	h	m		d	h	m
Perihelion	Jan	04	14	Equinoxes	Mar	20	10	29	Sept	22	20	02
Aphelion	July	03	20	Solstices	June	21	04	24	Dec	21	16	28

If you enjoyed the photographs shown in this calendar then please be sure to check out our website. It can be found at http://danwiz.com. As long as he is alive he hopes to be able to maintain it.

Kazuya's blog can be found at: http://studiesofplantsandwildlife.blogspot.com or alternately, http://www2.blogger.com/profile/02622643778290337101.

www.ingramcontent.com/pod-product-compliance
Lightning Source LLC
Chambersburg PA
CBHW042138030726
47599CB00002B/532